100 F: Recipes

Lev Well

CONTENTS

Aggie Banana recipe

Description
A delicious recipe for Aggie Banana, with vanilla ice cream, milk, bananas and butterscotch schnapps.

Ingredients
2 scoops vanilla ice cream
1 cup whole milk
2 sliced bananas
2 oz butterscotch schnapps

Instructions
Put bananas in an uncovered plastic bowl and freeze. Leave in the cold to form.
Mix ice cream, milk, and frozen bananas until smooth. Add Schnapps, blend, and pour in serving glass.

Serving
Highball Glass

****

Alaskan Orange recipe

Description
A delicious recipe for Alaskan Orange, with Van Der Hum® liqueur, brandy and vanilla ice cream.

Ingredients
2 oz Van Der Hum® liqueur
3/4 oz brandy
4 tbsp vanilla ice cream

Instructions
Blend briefly all ingredients with a half glassful of crushed ice. Serve in a wine goblet. Serve with grated orange zest, chocolate and nutmeg

Serving
Wine Goblet
****

Alaskan Polar Bear recipe

Description
A delicious recipe for Alaskan Polar Bear, with amaretto almond liqueur, Frangelico® hazelnut liqueur, cocoa cream, chocolate syrup, ice cream and whipped cream.

Ingredients
1 oz amaretto almond liqueur
1 oz Frangelico® hazelnut liqueur
1 oz cocoa cream
1 oz chocolate syrup
1 scoop ice cream
1 1/2 oz whipped cream

Instructions
Mix ingredients until of milkshake consistency. Place in a highball glass. Enjoy with whipped cream.

Serving
Highball Glass
****

Alcoholic Icy-Pole recipe

Description
A delicious recipe for Alcoholic Icy-Pole, with passion-fruit juice and vodka.

Ingredients
passion-fruit juice
vodka

Instructions
Blend the ingredients, put into an icy-pole template, and freeze. Serve on a hot day.
****

Apple a la Mode recipe

Description
A delicious recipe for Apple a la Mode, with dark rum, apple juice and vanilla ice cream.

Ingredients
1 oz dark rum
2 oz apple juice
1 tbsp vanilla ice cream

Instructions
Mix briefly all ingredients with half a glassful of crushed ice. Deliver in a double cocktail glass with a sprig of mint.

Serving
Cocktail Glass

****

Banana Colada #2 recipe

Description
A delicious recipe for Banana Colada #2, with light rum, banana, vanilla ice cream, pineapples, pina colada mix and ice.

Ingredients
1 1/2 oz light rum
1/2 banana
1 scoop vanilla ice cream
1 tsp crushed pineapples

1 1/2 oz pina colada mix
ice

Instructions
Blend in a blender all the ingredients except for the ice. After that add ice so that the drink begins to thicken. Serve.
****

Banana Foster recipe

Description
A delicious recipe for Banana Foster, with vanilla ice cream, spiced rum, banana liqueur and banana.

Ingredients
2 scoops vanilla ice cream
1 1/2 oz spiced rum
1/2 oz banana liqueur
1 banana

Instructions
Mix until soft and serve in a large brandy snifter. Spread cinnamon on top.

Serving
Brandy Snifter

****

Banana Nutbread recipe

Description
A delicious recipe for Banana Nutbread, with Frangelico® hazelnut liqueur, creme de bananes, dry sherry and vanilla ice cream.

Ingredients
1 oz Frangelico® hazelnut liqueur
1 oz creme de bananes
1/2 oz dry sherry
1 tbsp vanilla ice cream

Instructions
Blend all ingredients briefly with half a glassful of crushed ice.
Pour in a double-cocktail glass and serve.

Serving
Cocktail Glass

****

Batidas Frozen recipe

Description
A delicious recipe for Batidas Frozen, with cachaca, tropical-fruit
puree, condensed milk and simple syrup.

Ingredients
2 oz cachaca
2 oz tropical-fruit puree
1 oz sweetened condensed milk
1 oz simple syrup

Instructions
Mix all ingredients and ice and pour into an old-fashioned glass.
Decorate the drink with a lime wheel. Serve.

Serving
Old-Fashioned Glass
****

Blueberry Freeze recipe

Description
A delicious recipe for Blueberry Freeze, with vodka, wildberry schnapps, cream of coconut, blueberries, pineapples, vanilla ice cream, crushed ice and whipped cream.

Ingredients
1 oz vodka
1/4 oz wildberry schnapps
1 oz cream of coconut
2 oz blueberries
1 1/2 oz crushed pineapples
1 scoop vanilla ice cream
8 oz crushed ice
1 tbsp whipped cream

Instructions
Blend thoroughly all the ingredients and pour the mix into a specialty glass. Put whipped cream on the top. Use a teaspoon of blueberries to garnish.
****

Brandy Alexandra recipe

Description
A delicious recipe for Brandy Alexandra, with brandy, creme de cacao, vanilla ice cream, ice and cinnamon.

Ingredients
1 oz brandy
1/2 oz creme de cacao
1 scoop vanilla ice cream
1 scoop ice
powdered cinnamon

Instructions
Combine all ingredients in your blender. Blend. Garnish the drink with cinnamon powder.
****

Brazilian Monk recipe

Description
A delicious recipe for Brazilian Monk, with Frangelico® hazelnut liqueur, Kahlua® coffee liqueur, dark creme de cacao, dry sherry and vanilla ice cream.

Ingredients
1 oz Frangelico® hazelnut liqueur
1 oz Kahlua® coffee liqueur
1 oz dark creme de cacao
1/2 oz dry sherry
4 tbsp vanilla ice cream

Instructions
Put all ingredients into a serving glass and blend briefly. Garnish with a mint leaf and cherry, and dust with grated chocolate.

Serving
Collins Glass

****

Brute recipe

Description
A delicious recipe for Brute, with amaretto almond liqueur, dark creme de cacao and vanilla ice cream.

Ingredients

1 oz amaretto almond liqueur
1 oz dark creme de cacao
3 tbsp vanilla ice cream

Instructions
Put all ingredients in a Collins glass. Mix with half a glass of crushed ice. Blend briefly. Put a cherry on top. Serve. Use straws.

Serving
Collins Glass

****

Butter Pecan recipe

Description
A delicious recipe for Butter Pecan, with Frangelico® hazelnut liqueur, vanilla ice cream and pecan nuts.

Ingredients
1 oz Frangelico® hazelnut liqueur
2 tbsp vanilla ice cream
5 pecan nuts

Instructions
Pour frangelico liqueur into a serving glass. Add ice-cream. Chop coarsely the pecan nuts and place them in the glass.

Serving
Cocktail Glass

****

Cherry Chocolate Freeze recipe

Description
A delicious recipe for Cherry Chocolate Freeze, with cherry brandy, dark creme de cacao, chocolate syrup and vanilla ice

cream.

Ingredients
1 oz cherry brandy
1 oz dark creme de cacao
1/2 oz chocolate syrup
2 tbsp vanilla ice cream

Instructions
Put half a glassful of crushed ice in a wine glass. Also put all the ingredients in the glass. Blend briefly. Decorate with a cherry and a sprig of mint. Spread grated chocolate, add straws, and serve.

Serving
White Wine Glass

****

Cherry Tree Climber recipe

Description
A delicious recipe for Cherry Tree Climber, with cherry brandy, white creme de cacao, peppermint schnapps and vanilla ice cream.

Ingredients
1 oz cherry brandy
1 oz white creme de cacao
1/2 oz peppermint schnapps
1 tbsp vanilla ice cream

Instructions
Put half a glassful of crushed ice in a blender. Also put all the ingredients in the glass. Blend the mixture briefly. Pour into a cocktail glass and serve.

Serving
Cocktail Glass

****

Cocobanana recipe

Description
A delicious recipe for Cocobanana, with white rum, creme de bananes, amaretto almond liqueur, coconut rum, pineapple juice, coconut cream, banana and vanilla ice cream.

Ingredients
1 oz white rum
1 oz creme de bananes
1/2 oz amaretto almond liqueur
1/2 oz coconut rum
3 oz pineapple juice
1 oz coconut cream
1/3 mashed banana
3 tbsp vanilla ice cream

Instructions
Put half a glassful of crushed ice in a pina colada glass. Also add all ingredients to the glass. Blend the mixture briefly. Garnish with fruit. Add straws. Serve.

Serving
Pina Colada Glass

****

Country Cream recipe

Description
A delicious recipe for Country Cream, with coffee liqueur, pear liqueur, Campari® bitters, raspberry liqueur and vanilla ice cream.

Ingredients
1 oz coffee liqueur
1 oz pear liqueur
1/2 oz Campari® bitters
1/3 oz raspberry liqueur
3 tbsp vanilla ice cream

Instructions
Put half a glassful of crushed ice in a wine glass. Also add all the ingredients in the glass. Blend the mixture briefly. Put straws in the glass and serve.

Serving
White Wine Glass

****

Creamsicle Margarita recipe

Description
A delicious recipe for Creamsicle Margarita, with gold tequila, orange juice, sweet and sour mix, vanilla ice cream and crushed ice.

Ingredients
1 1/4 oz gold tequila
3 oz orange juice
1 oz sweet and sour mix
1 scoop vanilla ice cream
6 oz crushed ice

Instructions
Put all the ingredients in a blender. Blend the mixture until slushy. Pour in a serving glass.

Serving
Margarita Glass

****

Creamy Grasshopper recipe

Description
A delicious recipe for Creamy Grasshopper, with white creme de cacao, green creme de menthe and vanilla ice cream.

Ingredients
3/4 oz white creme de cacao
3/4 oz green creme de menthe
2 scoops vanilla ice cream

Instructions
Blend until smooth. The consistency of the drink should be thick, shake-like.

Serving
Hurricane Glass

****

Crime of Passion recipe

Description
A delicious recipe for Crime of Passion, with dark rum, passion-fruit juice, vanilla ice cream, raspberry syrup and cream soda.

Ingredients
1 oz dark rum
1 oz passion-fruit juice 2 tbsp vanilla ice cream 1/3 oz raspberry syrup 3 oz cream soda

Instructions
Blend all ingredients briefly. Pour into a serving glass and add cream soda. Use a slice of orange and a cherry to garnish.

Serving
White Wine Glass

****

Dirty Banana recipe

Description
A delicious recipe for Dirty Banana, with creme de bananes, creme de cacao, Kahlua® coffee liqueur and vanilla ice cream.

Ingredients
1 oz creme de bananes
1 oz creme de cacao
1 oz Kahlua® coffee liqueur
2 scoops vanilla ice cream

Instructions
Take six ice cubes and blend with ice-cream in a blender until smooth. Pour liqueur and blend again until smooth. If the mixture is not of milk-shake consistency, add more ice-cream. Pour into a serving glass.

Serving
Highball Glass
****

Florida Pina Colada recipe

Description
A delicious recipe for Florida Pina Colada, with pineapple juice, vanilla ice cream, coconut rum, dark rum, orange juice, cream and ice cubes.

Ingredients
3 oz pineapple juice
2 scoops vanilla ice cream
3/4 oz coconut rum
3/4 oz dark rum
2 splashes orange juice
3/4 oz cream
2 ice cubes

Instructions
Blend all ingredients in a blender for 1 minute or until smooth. Serve immediately.

Serving
Hurricane Glass

****

Friesian recipe

Description
A delicious recipe for Friesian, with amaretto almond liqueur, Frangelico® hazelnut liqueur, vanilla ice cream and chocolate syrup.

Ingredients
1 oz amaretto almond liqueur
1 oz Frangelico® hazelnut liqueur
3 tbsp vanilla ice cream
1 tsp chocolate syrup

Instructions
Put all ingredients in a collins glass. Mix with half a glassful of crushed ice. Blend briefly. Put a cherry on top.

Serving
Collins Glass

****

Frozen Barcelona recipe

Description
A delicious recipe for Frozen Barcelona, with Spanish brandy, Dry Sack® sherry, Cointreau® orange liqueur, orange juice, heavy cream and simple syrup.

Ingredients
3/4 oz Spanish brandy
3/4 oz Dry Sack® sherry
3/4 oz Cointreau® orange liqueur
3/4 oz fresh orange juice
3/4 oz heavy cream
1 oz simple syrup

Instructions
Put in a blender all ingredients and 3/4 cup of crushed ice. Blend. Pour into a sherry glass. Lightly dust with cinnamon. Serve.

Serving
Sherry Glass
****

Frozen Coconut recipe

Description
A delicious recipe for Frozen Coconut, with white rum, coconut rum and coconut ice cream.

Ingredients
1 1/2 oz white rum
1 oz coconut rum
3 tbsp coconut ice cream

Instructions
Blend briefly all ingredients together with half a glassful of crushed ice. Decorate with a sprig of mint. Use straws, and serve.
****

Frozen Fruit Daiquiri recipe

Description
A delicious recipe for Frozen Fruit Daiquiri, with white rum, dark rum, syrup, powdered sugar, fruit and lime juice.

Ingredients
2 oz white rum
2 - 3 dashes dark rum
2 - 3 dashes syrup
1/2 tsp powdered sugar
fruit pieces
3/4 oz lime juice

Instructions
Combine all ingredients in a blender, and blend. Pour the cocktail into a serving glass. Use the following fruits: bananas, pineapples and strawberries.

Serving
Cocktail Glass
****

Frozen Key Lime recipe

Description
A delicious recipe for Frozen Key Lime, with white rum, dark rum, lime juice and vanilla ice cream.

Ingredients
1 oz white rum
1/2 oz dark rum
1 1/2 oz lime juice
3 tbsp vanilla ice cream

Instructions
Combine in a wine goblet all ingredients with half a glassful of crushed ice. Blend briefly. Decorate with a slice of lime and a cherry, and serve.

Serving
Wine Goblet

****

Frozen Mudslide #2 recipe

Description
A delicious recipe for Frozen Mudslide #2, with rum, Kahlua® coffee liqueur, Irish cream, vanilla ice cream and chocolate syrup.

Ingredients
2 oz rum
2 oz Kahlua® coffee liqueur
2 oz Irish cream

2 cups vanilla ice cream
1 oz chocolate syrup

Instructions
Pour all liquid ingredients into a mixer. Add vanilla ice cream and
mix. To get a desired texture, add more ice cream.
****

Frozen Strawberry Banana Colada recipe

Description
A delicious recipe for Frozen Strawberry Banana Colada, with
dark rum, coconut cream, strawberries,
banana and crushed ice.

Ingredients
1 1/4 oz dark rum
2 oz coconut cream
2 oz strawberries
1 medium banana
8 oz crushed ice

Instructions
Put together all ingredients in a blender and blend until smooth.
Pour into a serving glass. Decorate with a fresh strawberry. Serve.
****

Gamble recipe

Description
A delicious recipe for Gamble, with apricot brandy, Mandarine
Napoleon® orange liqueur, sweet sherry, mango juice and vanilla
ice cream.

Ingredients
1 oz apricot brandy
3/4 oz Mandarine Napoleon® orange liqueur
1/2 oz sweet sherry
1 oz mango juice
3 tbsp vanilla ice cream

Instructions
Combine in a wine goblet all ingredients with half a glassful of crushed ice. Blend briefly. Serve.

Serving
Wine Goblet
****

Glaciermeister recipe

Description
A delicious recipe for Glaciermeister, with vanilla ice cream, milk and Jagermeister® herbal liqueur.

Ingredients
2 scoops vanilla ice cream
1 shot milk
1 1/2 oz Jagermeister® herbal liqueur

Instructions
Combine the ice cream, milk and jagermeister in a blender. Blend until smooth.
****

Hammer Horror recipe

Description
A delicious recipe for Hammer Horror, with vodka, Kahlua®

coffee liqueur and vanilla ice cream.

Ingredients
1 oz vodka
1 oz Kahlua® coffee liqueur
4 tbsp vanilla ice cream

Instructions
Combine all ingredients in a highball glass. Blend briefly. Dust with grated chocolate. Serve with straws.

Serving
Highball Glass

****

Hummer recipe

Description
A delicious recipe for Hummer, with coffee liqueur, light rum and vanilla ice cream.

Ingredients
1 oz coffee liqueur
1 oz light rum
2 scoops vanilla ice cream

Instructions
Combine all ingredients in a blender. Blend at a low speed. Serve into a highball glass.

Serving
Highball Glass
****

Ice Cream Genius recipe

Description
A delicious recipe for Ice Cream Genius, with amaretto almond liqueur, orange juice and vanilla ice cream.

Ingredients
2 oz amaretto almond liqueur
1/2 cup orange juice
1/2 cup vanilla ice cream

Instructions
Blend all ingredients together in a blender.

Serving
Cocktail Glass

****

Iceberg In Radioactive Water #2 recipe

Description
A delicious recipe for Iceberg In Radioactive Water #2, with Midori® melon liqueur, banana liqueur, ice cream, vodka, pineapple juice and Malibu® coconut rum.

Ingredients
2 shots Midori® melon liqueur
2 shots banana liqueur
1 shot vodka
fill with pineapple juice
1 shot Malibu® coconut rum
1 scoop ice cream

Instructions
Add to the serving mug all the ingredients in the sequence above. The ice cream is last.

Serving
Beer Mug

****

Iceberg in Radioactive Water recipe

Description
A delicious recipe for Iceberg In Radioactive Water, with Midori® melon liqueur, Malibu® coconut rum, banana liqueur, pineapple juice and vanilla ice cream.

Ingredients
3 oz Midori® melon liqueur
1 oz Malibu® coconut rum
1 oz banana liqueur
6 - 8 oz pineapple juice
1 scoop vanilla ice cream

Instructions
Pour all drinks into a glass. After that, add ice-cream.
****

ABOUT ICE CREAMS

Giving recipes for ice creams and the like in a book given to telling of beverages would seem a queer conceit, were it not for the fact that ice creams, sherbets and water ices are often used to quench the thirst; this is my reason and my only excuse, should an excuse be needed.

Vanilla Ice Cream

Ingredients
1 quart of cream,
¾ cupful of honey,
1 cupful of milk,
1 tablespoonful of vanilla extract.

Instructions
Heat the milk, add the honey, and stir until melted and thoroughly mixed. Allow to cool somewhat; add the cream, vanilla and a pinch of salt (a very small pinch), and freeze.
****

Vanilla Ice Cream (French)

Ingredients
2 cupfuls of scalded milk,
1 cupful of sugar,
3 eggs
$1/_8$ teaspoonful of salt,
1   quart of thin cream,
2   tablespoonfuls of vanilla.

Instructions
Make a custard of the first four ingredients. Strain and cool the custard and add to it the cream and vanilla. Freeze until firm, then pack in ice and salt.
****

Inexpensive Ice Cream

Ingredients
1¼ cupfuls of sugar,
1   quart of milk,
2   tablespoonfuls of cornstarch,
3   eggs,

Instructions
Desired extract and a pinch of salt.
Heat the milk, add the syrup and the cornstarch, which should have been moistened with a little cold milk; cook until it begins to thicken, add a pinch of salt and the beaten eggs. Boil, strain, cool and freeze.
With this as a foundation one may add any flavoring desired, or any crushed fruit. Coffee or chocolate may also be used. Very strong coffee is needed, but the amount of milk should be reduced in proportion.
****

Pistachio Ice Cream

Ingredients
2 cupfuls of scalded milk,
1 tablespoonful of flour,
1 cupful of sugar,
1 egg,
⅛ teaspoonful of salt,
1 quart thin cream,
1 tablespoonful of vanilla extract,
1 teaspoonful of almond extract.

Instructions
Mix flour, sugar and milk, add egg, slightly beaten, and milk gradually. Cook until it has the consistency of a soft custard. Let

this custard cool and add cream and flavoring, color with leaf green; strain and freeze.
****

Orange Ice Cream

Ingredients
2 cupfuls of sugar,
1 cupful of water,
2 cupfuls of orange juice,
¼ cupful of candied orange peel,
1 cupful of cream,
2 egg yolks,
1 cupful of double cream.

Instructions
Boil the water and sugar eight minutes. Add the orange juice. Make a custard of the cream and egg yolks. Cool and add to the first mixture with the heavy cream beaten stiff. Freeze. When nearly frozen add the orange peel. The dish is given a " different " look if it is served with candied orange peel.
****

Marshmallow Ice Cream

Ingredients
1½ cupfuls of milk,
½ cupful of heavy cream,
⅛ cupful of sugar,
1 junket tablet,
1 tablespoonful cold water,
2 heaping tablespoonfuls of marshmallow cream,
1 tablespoonful of vanilla.

Instructions

Put milk, cream and sugar into the can of freezer. Set in hot water until luke warm, add junket tablet dissolved in cold water, and allow to stand until firm. Add vanilla and marshmallow cream, mix thoroughly and freeze, using three parts ice to one part salt.

****

Frozen Pudding

Ingredients

1 pint of milk,
1 cupful of sugar,
3 eggs,
1 teaspoonful of cornstarch,
$\frac{1}{8}$ teaspoonful of salt,
1 pint thin cream,
½ teaspoonful of vanilla,
1 cupful of diced marshmallows,
1 cupful of thinly sliced peaches,
1 cupful of shredded pineapple,
1 cupful crystallized cherries.

Instructions

Beat the yolks of the eggs until very light, add sugar, cornstarch and salt. Beat into this the scalded milk, place in a double boiler and cook until it will coat the spoon. Remove from the fire and when cold add the cream, vanilla and stiffly beaten whites of the eggs. Pour into a freezer, add the marshmallows and fruit and freeze until firm, then pack and allow to stand for several hours.

****

Cocoanut Ice Cream

Ingredients

4 cupfuls of milk,

2½ tablespoonfuls of cornstarch,
2 eggs,
¾ cupfuls of honey,
1 teaspoonful of vanilla extract,
1   cupful of chopped fresh cocoanut or shredded
cocoanut, Preserved cherries,
Milk or water.

Instructions
Heat the milk in a double boiler. Blend the cornstarch with a little
milk or water and add to the hot milk and stir until it begins to
thicken. Add the beaten eggs and honey, cook for a minute or two ;
add vanilla and cocoanut. Freeze, serve in attractive tall stemmed
goblets; top with cocoanut and cherries.
****

Rose Ice Cream (With Condensed Milk)

Ingredients
2   cans of condensed milk,
3½ cupfuls of water,
2 teaspoonfuls of rose extract,
3 tablespoonfuls of cornstarch,
¼ cupful of milk, or water,
1 teaspoonful of vanilla,
1 teaspoonful of orange extract,
Red vegetable coloring.

Instructions
Mix one can of condensed milk with two cupfuls of water; add the
rose extract and enough red vegetable coloring to make the color
desired. Strain and freeze.
Boil the remaining water (1½ cupfuls) and stir in the other can of
condensed milk. Moisten the cornstarch with a little milk or water,
blend with the milk and water, stirring constantly for five or six

minutes. Allow to cool, add flavoring, strain and freeze. Place these creams in separate layers in a wet mold, place the cover on securely, pack and freeze. This should stand at least two hours.
****

Pineapple Ice Cream

Ingredients
1½ cupfuls of hot milk,
2 eggs,
½ cupful of honey,
2 cupfuls of shredded pineapple.
1 cupful of cream

Instructions
Beat the eggs, mix with the milk and honey; cook until smooth, stirring constantly. Allow to cool, add cream and freeze. When serving this cream, a generous spoonful of sweetened whipped cream is a delightful addition.
****

Strawberry Ice Cream

Description
This is not difficult to make and approaches the flavor of the fresh fruit more nearly than most creams in which fresh strawberries are used.

Ingredients
½ pint of thick cream,
1 pint of milk,
2 tablespoonfuls of cornstarch,
2 eggs,
3 tablespoonfuls of sugar,

½ teaspoonful of vanilla,
1 cupful of strawberry jam,
Small pinch of salt.

Instructions
Make a boiled custard of the milk, cornstarch, salt and the beaten eggs. Add the vanilla, cool and fold in a half pint of cream which has been whipped until stiff. Put in freezer and freeze slowly for five or six minutes; open
the freezer and stir in a full cupful of strawberry jam. Re-cover and continue to freeze until firm.
****

Green Tea Ice Cream

Ingredients
1 pint of milk,
1 tablespoonful of green tea,
1 pint of cream,
¾ cupful of sugar,
3 eggs,
½ teaspoonful of vanilla.

Instructions
Pour one pint of boiling milk over one tablespoonful of green tea, and allow to stand on the back of the range or on an asbestos mat over a low gas flame for five minutes; strain through a double thickness of fine cheesecloth. To this add the cream, beaten eggs, sugar and vanilla, and stir until it thickens. Add a little green vegetable color. Place in a cold dish and allow to cool. Freeze, repack, and allow to stand until ready for use.
****

Easy Peach Ice Cream

Ingredients
1 pint of peach pulp and the juice,
1 cupful of sugar,
1 quart of cream.

Instructions
Crush the peaches, using enough to make a pint of pulp. Save all the juice. Add the sugar to the juice and pulp; then add the cream, whipped as stiff as possible. Blend and freeze.
****

Some Unusual Frozen Dainties Coffee Parfait

Ingredients
1 pint of thick cream,
1½ cupfuls of confectioner's sugar,
½ cupful of strong coffee,
½ teaspoonful of vanilla,
½ teaspoonful of gelatine,
Milk.

Instructions
Dissolve the gelatine in two tablespoonfuls of milk, and pour the hot coffee over, stirring well; add sugar and vanilla. Fold in the cream, whipped stiff, pour into the freezer, pack in ice and salt and allow to stand for at least four hours.
Serve in attractive tall glasses, topped with a generous spoonful of sweetened whipped cream.
****

Apricot Parfait

Ingredients

1½ cupfuls of crushed apricots (canned or fresh),
2 tablespoonfuls of lemon juice,
¾ cupful of sugar,
1 teaspoonful of gelatine,
2 eggs,
1 cupful of thick cream.

Instructions

Mash the fruit and press through a fine sieve, add the lemon juice and sugar and heat until it reaches the boiling point, stirring constantly; beat the yolks of the eggs until very light and add slowly to the fruit mixture while hot; return to the fire and cook until a custard-like consistency. Dissolve the gelatine in a very little water and add to the fruit and eggs; allow to cool; chill; beat the whites of the eggs until stiff, and the cream until firm, and add both to the fruit mixture.

Pour into a mold, pack in ice and salt and allow to stand for several hours; serve in tall narrow glasses.

****

Cherry Parfait

Ingredients

1 cupful of thick cream,
²/₃ cupful of sugar,
¹/₃ cupful of water,
2 egg whites,
1 tablespoonful of gelatine,
¾ cupful of marshmallows,
1¼ cupfuls of stoned cherries (canned red cherries may be used),
1 cupful of cherry juice,
2 tablespoonfuls of lemon juice.

Instructions

Cut the marshmallows into very small pieces, and cut the cherries in halves; combine these with the cherry juice and allow to stand for two hours.

Boil the sugar and water until it will " spin a thread " and pour slowly over the stiffly beaten whites of the eggs, beating constantly. Allow it to become chilled, and stir in the stiffly whipped cream. Soak the gelatine in a little water and melt over hot water. Strain into the fruit mixture, beating briskly, until well blended; allow this to cool and when it begins to thicken, beat in the whipped cream. Pour into a wet mold, pack in ice, and salt, and allow to stand for three hours or more. Serve in parfait glasses, topped with whipped cream and a cherry.

****

Grape and Pineapple Parfait

Ingredients
2 cupfuls of milk,
2 egg whites,
1 cupful of sugar,
½ cupful of chopped nut meats,
¼ teaspoonful of powdered nutmeg,
4 cupfuls of pineapple juice,
Preserved grapes,
Whipped cream,
Rose extract,
Crystallized mint.

Instructions
The foundation of this delightful parfait is made in the following manner: Scald the two cupfuls of milk and add the beaten egg whites; stir in the sugar and chopped nuts. Cook until thick, add the nutmeg; cool and add the pineapple juice and freeze.
Put a spoonful of frozen mixture in the bottom of a tall glass, then a spoonful of preserved grapes, and fill the glass with the cream. Top with whipped cream which has been sweetened and flavored with rose. A crystallized mint adds to the attractiveness of this unusual parfait.

****

Raspberry Parfait

Ingredients
1 pint of cream,
1 pint of raspberries,
Sugar.

Instructions
Whip a pint of cream until very stiff, and sweeten with powdered sugar slightly. Cook the raspberries until broken, which should not take more than five or six minutes; press out all the juice and pulp possible, and reboil with three-fourths as much sugar as juice. Allow this to cool. Spread whipped cream in a mold, and pour some of the raspberry syrup over, and add more cream, and so fill the mold. Unless one prefers, then the syrup and whipped cream may be lightly mixed before packing in the mold. Pack in ice and salt and allow to stand for several hours

****

Maple Bisque

Ingredients
2 eggs,
½ pint of cream,
½ cupful of maple syrup,
Vanilla.

Instructions
Beat the yolks of the eggs until very light, add the maple syrup slowly, and heat over a slow fire, stirring constantly until it reaches the boiling point. Boil for one minute only; remove from the fire, strain and cool.

Beat the cream until firm and add to the stiffly beaten whites of the eggs. Pour the syrup mixture over this slowly, beating constantly; add the vanilla. Pour into a mold, pack and freeze.
****

Peach Melba

Ingredients
1 pint of heavy cream,
1 pint of milk,
1 cupful of sugar,
1 tablespoonful of gelatine,
½ teaspoonful of vanilla,
1 can of large peaches or ½ dozen selected peaches.

Instructions
Heat the milk and sugar, until the sugar is thoroughly dissolved; dissolve gelatine in a little cold milk and add to the heated milk and sugar.

Allow this to cool, add the cream whipped stiffly, flavor and pour into the freezer. Freeze until the crank turns very hard; remove the dasher, repack and allow to stand for two hours.

When ready to serve, place a half peach on the bottom of a long stemmed glass, fill with the cream, put the other half of the peach on top and top with raspberry syrup, then the whipped cream.

SAUCE.— To one cupful of raspberry jam add one cupful of boiling water sweetened a bit; boil for five minutes, strain, chill and use.
****

Peach Delight

Ingredients
2 cupfuls of water,
¾ cupful of honey,

1 teaspoonful of gelatine,
1 cupful of peach pulp,
1 lemon,
1 orange,
1 cupful of cream, whipped.

Instructions

Bring the water and honey to the boiling point and continue to cook for twenty minutes. Add the gelatine which should have been soaked and dissolved in a little cold water; strain and allow to cool. When cold add the peach pulp, orange pulp, orange juice and the juice of half a lemon. Turn into a freezer and freeze slowly. Serve in attractive glasses, topped with whipped cream.

Frozen Peaches

Ingredients

4 cupfuls of mashed peaches,
1½ cupfuls of sugar,
1 teaspoonful of lemon juice.

Instructions

Wipe the peaches with a damp cloth; pare and put the skins and one peach pit in two cupfuls of cold water and allow to boil for twenty minutes; strain through a sieve, pressing out all the juice; add the sugar, boil until the sugar is thoroughly dissolved and set aside to cool.

When cold add the mashed peaches and the lemon juice and freeze. If one wishes, a spoonful of whipped cream added to each serving adds perceptibly to this dainty.

****

Crushed Peaches

Ingredients
Peaches,
Sugar,
Cream.

Instructions
The housekeeper often finds that peaches are too ripe to slice and use with cream; in which case it is wise and economical to skin them, remove the stones and mash through a coarse sieve, adding sugar, honey or syrup to taste. If the peaches are the kind which have little flavor, a little lemon juice is desirable. Serve in low stemmed sherbet glasses, topped with whipped cream, on which a candied cherry may be placed,

Frosted Banana Cream

Ingredients
Bananas,
Sugar,
Lemon juice.

Instructions
Select only very ripe bananas; mash to a paste, sweeten with powdered sugar and flavor with a few drops of lemon juice. Press through a sieve and to each -cupful of banana add a half cupful of whipped cream. Mix and serve in attractive glasses, and sprinkle with powdered sugar.

■■■

ABOUT SORBETS, SHERBETS, WATER ICES, GRANITS
The difference in sorbets, sherbets, ices and granits is slight, still each fills its own particular purpose and place. Sorbets are supposed to be served after the meat course, and while the same

ingredients are used they are not frozen as long or as smooth as sherbets. Sherbets are smoother and firmer, and may well take the place of ice cream as a dessert. Water ices are made the same as sherbets, leaving out the egg whites. Granits are water ices frozen slightly; in fact so they will pour, and may be used as a drink.

Blackberry Sorbet

Ingredients
2   cupfuls of sugar syrup,
3   tablespoonfuls of lemon juice,
1   cupful of rich milk,
2   quarts of blackberries,
1   tablespoonful of gelatine,
2   egg whites.

Instructions
Press the berries through a sieve fine enough to keep the seeds from passing through, but pass the pulp through. Add one syrup and lemon juice. Dissolve the gelatine in a little water, and add to the berry juice and milk. Pour this mixture into the freezer and turn until it begins to thicken. Add the stiffly beaten whites of the eggs and continue to freeze until fluffy, but not so smooth as for sherbet. This is a fine distinction, but still it is considered worth differentiation.
When this " fluffy " stage is reached remove the dasher, repack and allow to stand for about two hours.
****

Plum Sherbet

Description
While any of these recipes may be made into either sherbet or sorbet, I will give from now on only the sherbet recipes.

Ingredients
1 quart of ripe plums (preferably red)
2 cupfuls of sugar syrup,
2 egg whites.

Instructions
Select only very ripe plums; wash, remove pits, and press through a sieve. There should be a pint of this pulp and juice. Add syrup, freeze until well thickened, add the stiffly beaten whites of the eggs, and continue to turn until frozen smooth and as hard as this sort of thing can well be frozen.
****

Cranberry Sherbet

Ingredients
1 quart of cranberries,
1 quart of water,
1 tablespoonful of gelatine,
1½ cupfuls of syrup,
1 egg white.

Instructions
Cook the cranberries in water for ten minutes. Press through a fine sieve, return to the saucepan and add the syrup, cook for five minutes, turn into the freezer, and when partly frozen, stir in the stiffly beaten white of an egg (use two egg whites if eggs are plentiful), and finish freezing.
****

Grapefruit Sherbet

Ingredients
2   cupfuls of water,
2 cupfuls of grapefruit juice,
1½ cupfuls of sugar,
1 teaspoonful of gelatine,
½ cupful of white grape juice,
1   egg white,
2   tablespoonfuls of chopped cherries.

Instructions
Boil the water and sugar together for ten minutes; soften the
gelatine with a little water and stir into this syrup.
Cool, add the juice of grapefruit and the grape juice. Turn into a
cold freezer and when the mixture begins to thicken well, add the
stiffly beaten white of an egg and the cherries (two egg whites are
better if eggs are not too expensive). Cover and freeze until firm
and smooth.
****

Grape Sherbet

Ingredients
1 teaspoonful of gelatine,
¾ cupfuls of grape juice,
1 cupful of syrup or sugar,
½ cupful of honey,
2 tablespoonfuls of lemon juice,
½ cupful of water,
1 egg white.

Instructions
Soak the gelatine in a little cold water; boil the syrup, honey and
half cupful of water, and add the dissolved gelatine. Allow this to

cool, add grape juice and the lemon juice and freeze. Open the freezer when slightly hard and add the stiffly beaten egg white. Re-cover and freeze until smooth and hard. (Two egg whites are better if plentiful.)
****

Creole Lemon Sherbet

Ingredients
3 lemons,
1 cupful of sugar,
2 cupfuls of water,
1 egg white.

Instructions
Boil the water and sugar, and add the grated rind of one lemon. Cool, add the juice of three lemons, strain through a fine cloth, and freeze until partly frozen, remove the cover, add the egg white stiffly beaten. Cover again and freeze until smooth.
****

Milk Sherbet

Ingredients
2 lemons,
1 cupful of syrup,
3 cupfuls of whole milk,
Candied cherries.

Instructions
Mix the juice of the lemons and the syrup, add the milk very slowly, stirring constantly, as it will curdle if poured too fast. That will not spoil the sherbet, but it does not look so well and one's appetite is helped by the appearance of one's food.

Freeze the mixture, serve in attractive glasses, with a few chopped candied cherries.
****

Orange Sherbet

Ingredients
1 egg white,
2 cupfuls of orange juice,
2 tablespoonfuls of lemon juice,
1 cupful of water,
¾ cupfuls of sugar (brown sugar or syrup may be used).

Instructions
Put the sugar in a saucepan with the water, bring to the boiling point, then cool. Add the orange and lemon juice, a pinch of salt and freeze.
Before the freezing is complete, add the egg white beaten stiffly; repack and continue to freeze until smooth.
****

Strawberry Sherbet

Ingredients
1 quart of strawberries,
2 cupfuls of water,
1 tablespoonful of lemon juice,
¾ cupfuls of syrup or sugar,
1 egg white.

Instructions
Wash and hull the strawberries, mash well and press through a cheesecloth. Add the syrup, lemon juice and water. Mix well,

freeze partially, add the stiffly beaten egg white, and finish
freezing.
****

Raspberry Sherbet

Ingredients
1 quart of raspberries,
1 egg white,
3 cupfuls of water,
1 cupful of syrup or sugar,
2 tablespoonfuls of lemon juice,
2 cupfuls of raspberry juice.

Instructions
Mash the berries and press through a cheesecloth; pour boiling
water over the the syrup; add the berry juice and lemon juice and
freeze. When partially frozen, add the stiffly beaten egg white, stir
in well, and continue to freeze until smooth.
****

Emergency Peach Sherbet

Instructions
This might also be called an economical sherbet, for one may use
just as many peaches as one has. For in this recipe one is supposed
to use peaches too ripe for slicing.
Mash the peaches, and press through a coarse sieve and sweeten to
taste. Half fill sherbet glasses with finely shaved ice and pour the
sweetened peach pulp over. Top each serving with a preserved or
candied cherry.
****

Pineapple Sherbet

Ingredients
1½ pints of grated pineapple,
1½ cupfuls of syrup,
1 tablespoonful of gelatine,
1 pint of rich milk,
2 egg whites.

Instructions
To the grated pineapple (canned may be used if fresh pineapple is not in season) add the syrup and the gelatine which has been dissolved in a small amount of water. Stir, pour into the chilled freezer, and freeze until about half frozen; open the freezer and add the milk; again turning the freezer until it turns with difficulty. Uncover, add the stiffly beaten whites of the eggs, turn until well mixed, and thoroughly hard.
If the dasher is removed and the sherbet repacked and allowed to stand to " ripen " for two hours, there will be a decided improvement in flavor and texture.
****

Tea Sherbet

Ingredients
2 cupfuls of tea,
1 cupful of sugar,
1 lemon,
1 orange,
½ cupful of water.

Instructions
Melt the sugar in the water and allow to begin to boil; take from the fire and add the juice of the lemon and orange; stir well, add the tea and freeze.

Apple Ice

Ingredients
1 quart of tart red apples,
1½ cupfuls of maple sugar,
3 cupfuls of water,
1 tablespoonful of lemon juice.

Instructions
Wash, quarter and remove the core, but do not pare the apples. Put them into a saucepan with the water; boil rapidly until soft. Mash and add the maple sugar. When cold press through a fine sieve, add the lemon juice and freeze.
****

Lemon Ice

Ingredients
1 cupful of sugar,
3 lemons,
Water.

Instructions
Add a cupful of sugar to the zest of one lemon and the juice of three; add enough water to make a quart. Allow this to come to the boiling point, cool, strain and freeze.
****

Loganberry Ice

Ingredients
2 cupfuls of loganberry juice,
1 cupful of sugar,
1 tablespoonful of lemon juice.

52

Instructions

Boil the water; add the sugar and when cold add the lemon and loganberry juices. Freeze until smooth and hard. Repack and allow to stand for two hours.

****

Strawberry Ice

Ingredients

1 cupful of sugar,
1 cupful of water,
1 quart of strawberries.

Instructions

Boil the sugar and water until it bubbles. Wash and hull the strawberries; mash and press through a cheesecloth. When the syrup is cold, add the strawberry juice and pulp; mix well and freeze.

****

Watermelon Ice

Ingredients

Ripe melon,
1½ cupfuls of sugar,
2 oranges,
1 lemon,
½ cupful of white grape juice,
Pink vegetable coloring.

Instructions

Remove the pulp from a ripe melon; press it through a fine sieve and add the sugar, lemon juice, orange juice and the zest of one orange and the grape juice. Color with enough vegetable color to make it a real watermelon pink; pack and freeze.

■■■ ■■ ■■

ABOUT FRUIT GRANITS
Granits are really " snow waters," frozen only enough to admit being poured. The granits are frozen in a freezer, although the Creoles usually freeze them in the " old fashioned water jugs."

Orange Granit

Ingredients
1½ cupfuls of orange juice,
½ pound of sugar,
1 pint of water

Instructions.
Peel six oranges very carefully, removing all the inner white part of the skin, and slice very thin. Place this in a deep bowl and sprinkle granulated sugar, allowing it to stand for five hours. Squeeze the juice from six oranges, and press the juice from the sliced ones, straining it and mixing the plain juice with this syrup. Add the water, strain and pour into a freezer; and freeze until like mush. Serve in small punch glasses.
****

Lemon Granit

Ingredients
1 pint of water,
½ pound of sugar,
1 cupful of lemon juice.

Instructions
Extract the juice from the lemons, add the sugar and stir until dissolved; add the water and freeze until mush-like and serve in attractive punch glasses.
****

Strawberry Granit

Ingredients
1 quart of strawberries,
1 tablespoonful of strawberry extract,
1 tablespoonful of lemon juice,
1 pound of sugar,
1½ pints of water.

Instructions
Crush the berries and cover with the sugar, allowing this to stand for five hours. Strain and press through a sieve, pressing out all the juice possible. Add the lemon juice, water and the extract. Turn this into a freezer and freeze until like mush. Serve in punch glasses.
****

Raspberry Granit

Ingredients
1 quart of raspberries, 1 tablespoonful of raspberry extract, 1 pound of sugar, ½ cupful of currants, 1 pint of water.

Instructions
Crush the currants and raspberries and cover with the sugar, allowing this to stand for five hours. Press through a sieve, being sure to leave no juice which can possibly be pressed out. Add the extract and water and freeze until like mush. Serve in punch glasses.

Ice-Cream Flip recipe

Description
A delicious recipe for Ice-Cream Flip, with triple sec, maraschino liqueur, vanilla ice cream, egg and nutmeg.

Ingredients
1 oz triple sec
1 oz maraschino liqueur
1 scoop vanilla ice cream
1 whole egg
nutmeg

Instructions
Combine all ingredients except nutmeg in a shaker. Shake and strain into a serving glass. Spread nutmeg on top. Serve.

Serving
Margarita Glass

****

Island Delight recipe

Description
A delicious recipe for Island Delight, with cherry vodka, white rum, dark rum, vanilla ice cream, whipped cream and grenadine syrup.

Ingredients

1 oz cherry vodka
1/2 oz white rum
1/2 oz dark rum
3 tbsp vanilla ice cream
1 oz whipped cream
1 teaspoon grenadine syrup

Instructions

In a wine goblet combine vodka, rums, ice cream and half a
glassful of crushed ice. Blend briefly. Place whipped cream on top.
Add a drop of grenadine and serve.

Serving

Wine Goblet

****

Jamaican Banana recipe

Description

A delicious recipe for Jamaican Banana, with light rum, creme de
cacao, creme de bananes, vanilla ice cream and banana.

Ingredients

1/2 oz light rum
1/2 oz creme de cacao
1/2 oz creme de bananes
2 scoops vanilla ice cream
1 sliced banana

Instructions

Combine all ingredients except for sliced banana in a blender.
Blend at a low speed. Pour the drink into a large brandy snifter.
Add sliced banana. Sprinkle with nutmeg. Put whole strawberry on

top. Serve.

Serving
Brandy Snifter

****

Liquid Courage recipe

Description
A delicious recipe for Liquid Courage, with milk, ice cream, creme de cacao, vodka and Bacardi® white rum.

Ingredients
1 pint milk
4 - 6 scoops ice cream
8 - 12 oz creme de cacao
6 oz vodka
6 oz Bacardi® white rum

Instructions
Combine all the ingredients in a blender and blend. Serve.
Serving
Beer Mug

****

Little Brother recipe

Description
A delicious recipe for Little Brother, with Kahlua® coffee liqueur, vodka, ice cream and vanilla extract.

Ingredients

2 oz Kahlua® coffee liqueur 1 oz vodka
1 scoop ice cream
1 tsp vanilla extract

Instructions
Put all the ingredients into a blender. Add an ice cube. Mix
thoroughly and serve.

Serving
Old-Fashioned Glass
****

Mexican Mudslide recipe

Description
A delicious recipe for Mexican Mudslide, with Kahlua® coffee
liqueur, amaretto almond liqueur, ice cream, whipped cream,
chocolate syrup and cherry.

Ingredients
1 oz Kahlua® coffee liqueur
1 oz amaretto almond liqueur
5 oz ice cream
1 1/2 oz whipped cream
chocolate syrup
1 cherry

Instructions
Mix the kahlua, amaretto and ice-cream in a glass. Beat chocolate
into the glass and top with whipped cream.
****

Monkey La La recipe

Description
A delicious recipe for Monkey La La, with vodka, Kahlua® coffee liqueur, half-and-half, ice cream and cream of coconut.

Ingredients
1 oz vodka
1 oz Kahlua® coffee liqueur 4 oz half-and-half
1 scoop ice cream
2 oz cream of coconut

Instructions
Blend all ingredients until smooth and frothy. Serve.

Serving
Hurricane Glass

****

Moosemilk recipe

Description
A delicious recipe for Moosemilk, with white rum, dark rum, Kahlua® coffee liqueur, vanilla ice cream and strawberries.

Ingredients
1 oz white rum
1 oz dark rum
1 oz Kahlua® coffee liqueur
2 scoops vanilla ice cream
2 fresh strawberries

Instructions
Put all ingredients in a blender. Blend until smooth.
****

Multiple Orgasm Cajun Style recipe

Description
A delicious recipe for Multiple Orgasm Cajun Style, with dark rum, Kahlua® coffee liqueur, amaretto almond liqueur, creme de cacao, rum cream liqueur and ice cream.

Ingredients
2 oz dark rum
2 oz Kahlua® coffee liqueur
1 oz amaretto almond liqueur
1 oz creme de cacao
1 oz rum cream liqueur
ice cream

Instructions
Combine all ingredients with ice in a blender. Blend until smooth. Serve.
****

Nut Crusher recipe

Description
A delicious recipe for Nut Crusher, with Frangelico® hazelnut liqueur, chocolate syrup and vanilla ice cream.

Ingredients
1 1/2 oz Frangelico® hazelnut liqueur
1/2 oz chocolate syrup
1 tbsp vanilla ice cream

Instructions
Combine all ingredients with half a glassful of crushed ice in a serving glass. Blend briefly. Spread chopped hazelnuts. Serve.

Serving
Wine Goblet

****

Pensacola Bushwacker recipe

Description
A delicious recipe for Pensacola Bushwacker, with cream of coconut, Kahlua® coffee liqueur, Bacardi® black rum, creme de cacao, half-and-half and vanilla ice cream.

Ingredients
4 oz cream of coconut
2 oz Kahlua® coffee liqueur
1 oz Bacardi® black rum
1 oz creme de cacao
4 oz half-and-half
vanilla ice cream (optional)

Instructions
Combine all ingredients with two cups of ice in a blender. Blend until mixed. Serve.
****

Phoenix Paradise recipe

Description
A delicious recipe for Phoenix Paradise, with Vladivar® vodka, cranberry juice, mango juice, orange juice and ice cream.

Ingredients
25 ml Vladivar® vodka
50 ml cranberry juice
50 ml mango juice

50 ml orange juice
2 tbsp ice cream

Instructions
Blend all ingredients and 4 ice cubes in a blender for about 20 - 30 seconds. Pour into a serving glass.

Serving
Highball Glass

****

Raspberry Swirl recipe

Description
A delicious recipe for Raspberry Swirl, with vodka, amaretto almond liqueur, vanilla ice cream and Chambord® raspberry liqueur.

Ingredients
1 part vodka
1 part amaretto almond liqueur
2 cups vanilla ice cream
1 jigger Chambord® raspberry liqueur

Instructions
Put vodka, amaretto and ice cream in a blender. Mix well. Pour into a serving glass. Carefully add Chambord® liqueur. Swirl the cocktail with a straw or stirring stick. Serve.

Serving
Hurricane Glass
****

Royal Peaches and Cream recipe

Description
A delicious recipe for Royal Peaches and Cream, with DeKuyper®
Peachtree schnapps, Crown Royal® Canadian whisky, Cointreau®
orange liqueur, heavy cream and vanilla ice cream.

Ingredients
1 1/2 oz DeKuyper® Peachtree schnapps
1/2 oz Crown Royal® Canadian whisky
1/2 oz Cointreau® orange liqueur
1 1/2 oz heavy cream
2 scoops vanilla ice cream

Instructions
Put all ingredients in a blender. Blend until smooth. Pour into a
serving jar. Decorate with a fresh slice of peach. Serve.

Serving
Mason Jar

****

Silver Stallion Fizz recipe

Description
A delicious recipe for Silver Stallion Fizz, with vanilla ice cream,
gin and carbonated water.

Ingredients
1 scoop vanilla ice cream
2 oz gin
carbonated water

Instructions
Shake together gin, vanilla ice-cream and ice. Strain into a serving

glass. Add carbonated water, stir, and serve.

Serving
Highball Glass
****

Smooth Pineapple Daiquiri recipe

Description
A delicious recipe for Smooth Pineapple Daiquiri, with pineapples, light rum, limeade, vanilla ice cream and ice.

Ingredients
8 slices canned pineapples
6 oz light rum
6 oz can frozen limeade
2/3 cup vanilla ice cream
ice

Instructions
Add limeade and rum into a blender. Mix. After that add pineapple and ice cream. Blend well. With the blender continuing to run, add a few pieces of ice so that the mixture is smooth and thick and the blender is almost full. Serve.
****

Snow Blinder recipe

Description
A delicious recipe for Snow Blinder, with vodka, vanilla ice cream and lemonade.

Ingredients
2 oz vodka
2 scoops vanilla ice cream
1 glass lemonade

Instructions
Combine vodka and ice cream in a blender. Blend. Pour lemonade on top.

Serving
Cocktail Glass
****

Strawberry Dream recipe

Description
A delicious recipe for Strawberry Dream, with strawberries, strawberry schnapps, Bacardi® dark rum, cream, pineapple juice, ice cubes and vanilla ice cream.

Ingredients
3 strawberries
3/4 oz strawberry schnapps
3/4 oz Bacardi® dark rum
3/4 oz cream
3/4 oz pineapple juice
4 ice cubes
2 scoops vanilla ice cream

Instructions
Place all ingredients in a blender. Blend for about 1 minute or until the drink is smooth. Pour into a serving glass.
Serving
Hurricane Glass

****

The Dark Side recipe

Description
A delicious recipe for The Dark Side, with amaretto almond liqueur, Bacardi® 151 rum, dark creme de cacao, Kahlua® coffee liqueur, triple sec, vanilla ice cream and chocolate syrup.

Ingredients
3/4 oz amaretto almond liqueur
3/4 oz Bacardi® 151 rum
3/4 oz dark creme de cacao
3/4 oz Kahlua® coffee liqueur
3/4 oz triple sec
3 scoops vanilla ice cream
chocolate syrup

Instructions
Blend all ingredients in a blender. Pour into a serving glass. Optional ? You can frost the glass with chocolate syrup before pouring.

Serving
Highball Glass
****

White Cargo recipe

Description
A delicious recipe for White Cargo, with vanilla ice cream, white wine, maraschino cherries and gin.

Ingredients
1 scoop vanilla ice cream
1 dash white wine

1/2 oz maraschino cherries
2 1/2 oz gin

Instructions
Mix all ingredients in a blender until the drink is smooth. If necessary add a little extra wine. Serve in a chilled goblet.

Serving
Wine Goblet

****

White Dove recipe

Description
A delicious recipe for White Dove, with amaretto almond liqueur, white creme de cacao, ice cream, chocolate syrup and whipped cream.

Ingredients
3/4 oz amaretto almond liqueur
3/4 oz white creme de cacao
2 cups ice cream
chocolate syrup
1 1/2 oz whipped cream

Instructions
Put into a blender the pamaretto, cream de cacao and the ice cream. Blend until the mixture has a shake consistency. Line the inside of a serving glass with chocolate syrup. Pour cocktail into a brandy snifter and top with whipped cream. Put cherry on top.

Serving
Brandy Snifter

Made in United States
Cleveland, OH
10 June 2025

17631070R00039